HOW TO ROCK REDUNDANCY

Stop applying for jobs and start applying yourself!

Amanda Noble-Simmons

Kindle

PROLOGUE

My Catalyst

It's March 2002.

It's a really, really cold day. I'm in the middle of Leeds city centre, outside a plush, tall office building, a law firm. A prestigious law firm that I have worked at for the last 3 years as Marketing Manager.

I have just made it out of the door and halfway across the road. But the traffic is busy and cars whoosh by on either side, sloshing through puddles that the rain has made. I'm 32 years old, long brown hair, average build, pretty in the right light, a serious face, or 'resting bitch face' as they would say nowadays. I have a rain mac on, but I didn't have time to button it up, so it's flapping in the wind and turning a darker shade in the rain.

There is a directional bollard in the middle of the road island and I lean over onto it and cradle my heavily pregnant belly.

The rain, already drenching me, begins to slam into my back and I can smell the asphalt on the road and the car exhaust fumes as the cars continue relentlessly to pass by. Nobody stops, nobody sees me sobbing my heart out.

My head is pounding. My mind is racing, trying to push myself into action. To think straight. But all I can think about is the rain and how ridiculous I must look right now. I shout in my head 'why is nobody stopping for a pregant woman sobbing in the street!'.

I fumble about in my handbag until I can find my phone. It's slippery in my hands and my vision is blurred by my own tears and by the rain cascading down my head. I drop my handbag because I feel the need to cradle my baby with my other hand whilst trying to call my husband.

As my bag falls to the floor, a lipstick falls out and rolls into the road and is crushed by a passing car. 'Fitting' I have time to think. I dial the number. My husband, Craig is ex-Army. Blonde, handsome, a bit taller than me, he was an Army Physical Training Instructor and ex-GB Triathlete and, like me, very straightforward and military. He answers: "Hi Mand, how's it going?"

I can't talk. I try, but all he hears is me gasping for breath and the rain.

Craig says, "Amanda, are you ok? What's happening? Is it the baby? Where are you?"

I manage to gasp through my sobs and say, "I'm, I'm....outside...... my office".

Another car goes by so close the water spashes up over my shoes and I stare at them, blindly.

"Bloody hell, are you ok? Breathe Mand, tell me what's wrong."

I sniff and wipe my face and nose all over my wet sleeve. I try and pull myself together, but I'm in shock. "I'm sorry, don't worry. It's ok, it's not the baby."

"OK, good, good. Christ, you scared the shit out of me then. Well, what is it then?"

"I've just been made redundant."

Silence.

Yes, it was that bad. I felt bereaved. I was shocked. But this was the start of something that changed me, forever. For the better. And it could change you too.

Let me tell you how.

1 THE CATALYST

The sneeky little catalyst

There is nearly always a catalyst for change. Getting cancer, moving house, starting a new job, having a baby or finishing a degree. There are so many. But for some, change is a dirty word. Some people hate change and physcially and mentally cannot cope with it. Not me, I thrive on change and have done my whole life. But if you are not comfortable with change, how can you deal with it?

Most of us sit comfortably within our comfort zones, hence the name. It's human nature. But sometimes, we are thrust out of these comfort zones by catalysts outside of our control. Redundancy is definitely one of them. That is what happened to me. Three times actually. But by the 2nd time, I was already prepared; by the 3rd, I was a master. Move over Yoda.

I am what you might call one of life's 'grafters'. I had a dodgy childhood, a poor education (it was the 80's after all) and no direction in life until I joined the RAF at 18. This move transformed me, from a nobody into a somebody. In the RAF I was one of the lads (I'm female, but you know what I mean). I had a profession, money, banter, travel and respect. I loved it. Three-year tour of Cyprus, Ayia Nappa every night. What wasn't to love?

But for me, it wasn't enough. I wanted more money, more travel, more life experiences, and in 1994, the RAF was no longer providing that for me. So I left. Now for those of you who do not like change, you would probably have stayed in the RAF, done your 25 years and be retired now while I am still grafting! So being somebody that embraces and thrives on change is not always a good thing. It just helps to be able to manage, should change or a major catalyst happen to you. I'm also not saying that sticking to one profession, house, etc. is wrong, not at all. I just want to explain how you can proactively create and manage change in your life, should that be what you desire.

So I'd met the man I was going to marry, a fellow Yorkshireman. He was in the Army and he also wanted to leave the military to join the Fire Service. So I did what I have always done in life. I facilitated it. I helped him. I didn't know then, but I know now that I have always done this in my life. Made things happen, create opportunities, have fingers in many pies.

The reason I know now, is that I feared bad things happening and so was always preparing in some way, for the worse. And I was right. Bad things do happen in life and most of us are not prepared for them. I had somehow cultivated myself to always be prepared! I would have made an amazing Scout!

So how did I 'facilitate' or 'make it easy' for Craig to leave the Army? I got a job as a housekeeper that provided us with a home that came with the job and a free re-location to Yorkshire. This meant he didn't have to earn, whilst I worked, until there was a slot for him to join the Fire Service. I worked and, six months later, he joined the Fire Service. Sorted.

Looking back on my life, I'm 50 now. I can see that I have facilitated and many people, boyfriends, husbands, friends, my own children and, of course, myself get the job/career or life goal they want. It's just something that comes naturally to me, but it is also born of experience, and not all of it pleasant. Being made redundant three times, for starters, is not very pleasant, even when you are prepared for it. But it can't hurt to be prepared.

If you know of the film 'Slumdog Millionaire', I liken myself to the lead character. He is a poor child from Mumbai, who manages to win 'Who Wants to be A Millionaire' because of his life experiences. And it's true, it is my belief that you won't be a well-rounded human if you only stay in your village, or come fresh out of university without a callous on your hand, or a scar on your body. They are just part of your path. You need to travel, to live a little on the edge, to help others less fortunate, to volunteer, to try new hobbies. All these things make you a well-rounded individual who has stories to tell, experiences to relive and memories to draw upon.

How will this help you land you your dream job, I hear you ask. I'm getting to that.

But, back to my story.

So my husband is now working for the Fire Service. I have left the RAF and am now working as a housekeeper to a rich family. Life was good. But I no longer had a career. I had a job. It wasn't enough. I wanted more money, more travel and more life experiences (sound familiar?). So I left.

I went to college part-time to do shorthand. I thought I could become an executive PA (a mere secretary wasn't going to cut it for me!). Whilst there, I was put forward by the tutor for a job she had seen as a Marketing Assistant at the largest accountancy practice in the world.

I applied, I interviewed well and I got the job. How? You might ask.

The reason is multi-faceted. But in reality, I am a goal chaser. I didn't know this then, but I know it now. I need constant goals in life to keep me thriving. Getting that job was a goal. So I worked to get it. If you have been made redundant, then your goal will be to find a new source of income, be that a new job or starting a business.

But each step to finding a new job has its own mini goal s; a) get over being made redundant b) deciding on your direction c) doing something about it.

2 THE GOAL CHASER

And I hate football

How did a 24-year-old woman, who left school barely scraping 3 O-Levels, now have a job at one of the most presitgious accountancy practices in the world? I call it CLOUT. I'm from Yorkshire you see, so CLOUT is how I have managed to get the job I want. How I excel at most things I do and how I can help you achieve the same. I got that job because I had 'The Royal Air Force' on my CV, I had excelled on the shorthand course and shown my tutor I was best-in-class. That is why I was chosen for interview, and that is how I got the job (well that's one aspect).

Point to note here: It's better to have a shit job at an amazing firm, than a great job at a shit firm!

But back to CLOUT

And before I tell you what my CLOUT is, I should probably explain what I mean by a goal chaser. I'm driven by achieving goals. All my life people have said, "Wow, how do you do all that you do?", "How do you squeeze it all in?" My husband will say "Why can't you sit still for two minutes?"; my ex-husband might say, "The grass isn't always greener!". Well, maybe, but it's a different shade of green and I wanna see it!

If I am not planning my next career move, house sale or purchase, holiday or personal achievement, I am not satisfied. But this is me, it may not be you. You might be somebody who is satisfied with everything in life, except your job or job situation, and that is why you are here, right? And that's great. You may not be driven by achieving goals. And that's great too. But you are reading this book, so you must want something to change, or have had change thrust on you.

1. Have you been made redundant?
2. Are you long-term unemployed?
3. Are you looking for your first job?
4. Do you hate the job you are in and want to leave?
5. Are you frustrated by your job search?
6. Have you applied for 100s of jobs and got nowhere?

I'm guessing that you must fit into one of the above categories or, at the very least, you are curious to know how you can make a change in your life, be it a new job or something else.

But yes, yes. Goals.
I've scored more goals than Miroslav Klose (German footballer who scored 16 goals in a World Cup) and all I want to do is show you how you can score just one!

By 'Goals', I mean objectives, achievements or changes in life. I've had quite a lot and here are some:

GOALS met
11 jobs
2 marriages
4 children
64 house moves

GOALS not asked for but met and survived
1 divorce

1 cancer
2 miscariages
3 redundancies
and now 1 Coronavirus!

As I mentioned in Chapter 1, I am a grafter and you have to be-come one too. Your dream job isn't going to land in your lap, you have to cultivate it, you have to put in the work, the effort. Sitting and aimlessly applying for jobs just isn't going to cut it anymore. Finding a new position in life is a full time job. You are now CEO of your life! So a grafter you have to become.

I started working at an early age and was head chef on the Pull-man train in Yorkshire by age 14. I was skiving school to work on the train 2 days/nights a week and I loved it (it's also the reason why I only scraped 3 O-Levels). I prepped the food, scrubbed the floors and learned how to cook by watching the chef (my mum!) and trying it myself. By the time the head chef left, I was able to run that little mobile kitchen all by myself!

From my experiences on the Pullman train, I got a job as a chef at a pub in York. But that was never going to satisfy me and so, at 18, I joined the RAF. I learnt morse code and went off to Cyprus for 3 years.

That is where I met my first husband, Craig. You already know I left the RAF, did the shorthand course, got the job at the global accountancy practice.

So, there I was at that practice and have worked there for 5 years. I now see my department looking to recruit a Director. I see my first opportunit, my first goal at this firm that I wanted to achieve. I put forward a well-thought-out proposal (I still have that document if anyone wants to see it), I put it forward to my boss and waited expectantly. I got turned down. This did not go down well with me and put a downer on working there. I decided I wanted more money, more travel and more life experiences (sound familiar...again?), so having worked my way up the career ladder for 5 years and having my proposal turned down, I decided I had to leave.

Having had my proposal turned down, which at the time I felt was because I didn't fit into the big boys club, it was never going to work after that, so I moved to join a large and prestigious law firm in Leeds. I was paid more, had more responsibility and was living the dream.

Right up until 2002. If you read the Prologue, then you know what happened next.

(**exit left and read the Prologue if you haven't already**)

3 CHANGE AFOOT

I have new feet every day

So there I was. I was 6 months pregnant, standing in the rain, crying my eyes out. I was the main bread winner, about to give birth and therefore with no prospect of getting another job straight away.

What would you have done? How would you have felt? I couldn't afford not to work: we would lose the house if the mortgage wasn't paid and I was about to bring my first child into the world. Fuck!

So, I did what any other self-respecting redundee would do: I curled up into a ball of self pity for about a month, locked myself in a dark room, cried my eyes out, watched sad films, listened to sad songs and slowly ate my way through a year's supply of chocolate.

But then one day, just like a rainbow after a storm, I thought, why am I doing this to myself? This is supposed to be one of the happiest times of my life. My child is on its way and a job is surely just a job.

But no, it isn't in many cases, is it? It was my career, my livelihood, the thing that put a roof over our heads, food on the table and provided holidays and memories. It meant so much more for me and it probably does for you too.

So how do you move on?

Before any action, there is inaction. In order to move forward there has to be action. So to get to that point you have to greive. You have to cycle as fast as you can through the greiving process.

The Grief Graph (Flow Diagram doesn't ryhme!)

For me, the first time I was made redundant, it look me about 6 weeks to get from Loss to Recovery and Action. By the 3rd time I was made redundant it took me 24 hours. I hope that, by writing this book and sharing what I have learnt, if you are ever made redundant you too can get from point A to Z in 24 hours, or I will be generous and give you a week!

It's like taking stock, you have to try and cycle as quick as you can through the greiving process in order to move forward and start taking action. You have to be at the acceptance stage before you can move on. It's just down to grit, you just have to, because without it you will spiral down even further, be longer unemployed, start to hate yourself and lose interest in everything and everyone around you and we don't want that, do we? No.

So come on, start today, start with acceptance of your circumstances. You cannot change it, it's pointless being angry or feeling sorry for yourself, or feeling bitter towards your employer. You are where you are, so accept it.

If you have been made redundant it's a catalyst for change, for action, to move forward. It is not a rejection, it is not personal, it is not final. It's an opportunity for better things and I can honestly say with my hand on my heart that every bad thing that has happened to me has resulted in much better things coming my way.

As I mentioned, the first time I was made redundant it took me longer to cycle through the Grief Graph, but once I recoginsed I had accepted it and was able to move forward and take action, the next time I was made redundant, I moved to that point in 1 or 2 days and the next time 24 hours.

From that moment of acceptance I also vowed to myself that I would never again fall victim to a faceless, careless, corporate and, if I was ever able to work again at another firm, I would work on my own terms. OK, so that may sound bitter? It isn't it is putting myself and my own wellbeing ahead of those of the company. I think any company would probably agree with me, that a happy workforce is a more productive workforce.

This moving on to acceptence started with my own mindset. I just decided that I wasn't going to be a victim. I was going to lead my own path and even if I was ever made redundant again, I would hold my head high and just crack on with finding something else to do that would pay the bills. Somewhere in there, you have to find humility and lose any arrogance.

My goal in life from that moment onwards was to make myself financially independent, so that I wouldn't have to rely on any firm and be at their mercy, should they suddenly decide that they no longer needed me.

I said, "don't take it personally" and neither should they.

Little did I know then, the recession of 2008 and the Coronavirus of 2020 were heading our way!

But how was I supposed to become financially independent. I was the main breadwinner, and after 9 years in professional services marketing, if you had cut me in half you would have seen 'corporate' written inside me. I was trapped in that profession. I liked my job, but I didn't love it and I also couldn't leave it as I needed the money. So at that time, I thought I would just ride it out in the corporate legal world, but on my terms. These were:
* Never work overtime
* Take a full hour lunch break
* Learn to say 'no'
* Improve delegation skills
* Make work a part of my life, not my whole life

So my first little girl was born. And 4 weeks later I started a new job at another law firm in Leeds. I was paid more, I had more responsibility, I was living the dream (again). But it wasn't too many more years before I wanted more money, more travel and more life experiences (sound familiar?).

Now don't get me wrong, I'm not a greedy person. The money I earn, I have earned it. I give 110% to every single job I do. I am not one to spend hours gossiping with colleagues (did I mention I am an introvert?), I can touch type at mach 10 (that Executive PA course paid off)! I spend it on houses and holidays and clothes and food for my children. I give to charities and volunteer my time. I'm not greedy, it's just a desire to better myself, to chase goals, to achieve more in life. I think it also might be a hang up from doing so crap at school and not going to university. Whatever your reason, it doesn't matter, just as long as you have the drive, every-thing else will follow.

This drive and this 'preparedness' meant that whilst I was at my new law firm (and any job I've ever had for that matter) I always had my CV prepared and up-to-date with any new achievements, and my ear to the ground on any new openings.

One day an ad for a job caught my eye:

Marketing Technology Manager - Global Law Firm - Based in the Cayman Islands

Well, what is a girl to do? I set my laser vision on getting that job, convicing my husband to move to the other side of the world and, 2 months later, there we were.

Again, how did I manage this? 'CLOUT' and something I am going to introduce to you called the Career Cultivation C.H.A.R.T.

But don't skip to that page just yet, I've still got my life story to share with you.

4 MINDSET

Yada Yada

Before I explain about finding your clout, I want to cover part of the Grief Graph that comes about when you can finally accept the position you are in. It's Mindset. Yes, I know! Mindset. It's all well and good for me to say just get out of your bed and decide you are not going to be a victim of redundancy. It's hard, I know. And mindset has been talked about a lot and I mean A LOT in books, on TV, on LinkedIN, on training courses - everywhere you look there is a book on mindset. But this isn't one of them. I just want to touch upon the subject because you *do* need a positive mindset in order to achieve your dream goal.

Positive Mental Attitude (PMA), DOES bloody work! It's so important to be in the right frame of mind before any action takes place. Writing this book, for example, I've had it in my drafts for over a year, but today, I decided I'm going to start it properly. Why? Because today the sun was shining, I had the time to do it (thanks Coronavirus) and my brain was in the right frame of mind to get started.

They use PMA in the military: it makes you jump off high shit and out of planes and delve down deep holes. Speaking of which, did I tell you I was in the RAF? Well, one day we were on a training course potholing. Now, potholing in the military is not the same as potholing in civvy street. We have to abseil down a dark hole while they chuck cold water on your blistered hands that are clinging to the rope (no safety, just literally holding onto the rope) that is stopping you from plummeting 20 feet.

They take away all torches, provide minimal instructions and basically let you loose, one by one, down into the murky, damp depths. One by one, we all managed to fuck up and ended up lost, in a dead end, in the pitch black. Panicking.

I realised, in that moment, that I had to gather my inner strength to help the others who were crying and panicking. I had to take the lead. I had no clue where I was going either. I just felt that someone had to take charge of the situation in order to make us all feel better. By George, it worked. PMA - Positive Mental Attitude. We were rescued eventually. End of. Other sayings include 'fake it till you make it', which also works.

The other thing the Military taught me was the six P's.

Planning and Preparation Prevent Piss Poor Performance.

Excuse all the swearing, but I am ex-forces after all!

This has stood me in good stead my whole life. Prepare, Prepare, Prepare. You don't need to have a university degree to know not turn up to an interview late, or not to have researched the company, or not to have scoped out the venue and parking options at the venue, or washed your hair and ironed your clothes. Tell me I'm wrong, but these are all common sense, aren't they? I surely don't need to teach you that? But trust me, I have interviewed people who showed up late, didn't wash their hair and didn't research the company or the job description. Shame on them and needless to say, they didn't get the job.

So, where was I up to? Oh yes, I was languishing in the Cayman Islands. I really *was* living the dream there. Tax-free salary, good job, Caribbean lifestyle.

But then disaster struck. A catalyst. Divorce.

I won't go into details. My ex-husband and I are still good friends.

And, it's fine, it all turned out ok in the end. But it was another catalyst for change afoot.

Now I was a single mum of two girls living thousands of miles from my family. We loved living in the Carribean, but it's expensive and a long way from home. So I decided to move to Spain to be near my mum who lived and worked there. A plane ride later, we were sipping Sangrias and I was deciding what next to do. I thought I would take a year off work altogether and take stock.

But this is me, the goal chaser! Even then, I couldn't keep still and take a year off like I planned.

Was I sad? Did I feel sorry for myself? Yes. But, despite having no job, no husband, no home and no income, I still had a positive mindset, a good CV and clout.

But I get bored easily and after a month I had already started to look at my next options, my next goal.

I started to apply for jobs in the UK and staight away I was offered one as Marketing Manager at law firm in Essex. At the same time, however, I also wrote speculatively to every law firm in Gibraltar offering my services. You see, I had already gotten the bug for living abroad after 3 years in the RAF in Cyprus, followed by my time in Cayman and now living in Spain. I couldn't decide if I wanted to go back to the UK or not. So based on my offshore law firm experience I decided that perhaps Gibraltar might be a good halfway point between living abroad, but also being close to home. So here started my speculative writing path.

Writing speculatively, but cleverly, is one of the key points in the **CAREER CULTIVATION C.H.A.R.T**. which I will explain in more detail later.

I was worried about the girls' education, so while I was waiting to hear back from the Gibraltar firms, I took the job at the law firm in Essex, set up home in the UK and I started work 2 weeks later.

I hated being back in the UK and was very happy when one of my letters landed me an interview at the largest law firm in Gibraltar. I was offered the role of Marketing Director. But I didnt take them up on the offer right away. Why not? Well you will have to wait and see, because now I want to explain to you what **CLOUT** is. Or what it means to me.

5 CLOUT

Without clout, your'e nowt!

Have I mentioned I'm from Yorkshire? OK, so I've over-played that card. But I've mentioned clout quite a lot. Here is what I mean.

Never underestimate your clout. This is what you know, what you have experienced in life that can contribute to achieving your deam job. In Yorkshire we call it 'clout'; you might call it skills, achievements, savvy, smarts, motivation, competence, life! It's basically what makes up you!

informal
influence or power, especially in politics or business.
"I knew she carried a lot of clout"
synonyms:
influence · power · pull · weight · sway · leverage · control · say · mastery

Let me give you an example:

Let's say you are a pub landlord and you want to hire a chef. Would you rather employ a chef straight out of chef school, or somebody that has travelled the world, jobbing in kitchens in every continent, learning new and exotic ways of cooking? I know which I would prefer. And if you were fresh out of chef school *AND* had travelled and jobbed in kitchens in every continent, then you would be even more attractive!

But my point is, 'experience counts'. It counts for a great deal. This book, however, isn't a one size fits all. For example, if you want to hire a doctor, you would want a qualified doctor, not somebody that has travelled the world practicing being a doctor with no actual qualifications. So you get my point. What I advise is not suitable to every field of work. But it is relevant for most.

If you don't know what makes up you, write it down. Just think of anything that you are good at, that you enjoy, that you have experienced.

Here is a useful checklist:

1. What are you good at?
2. What do you like doing?
3. When was your last compliment? What was it for?
4. Where have you been in life?
5. What jobs or part-time jobs have you worked so far?
6. What skills have you learnt?
7. Who do you know?
8. Which countries have you visited?
9. What exeperiences have shaped you?
10. Have you volunteered?
11. Have you taken any short courses?
12. What hobbies do you enjoy or excel at?

These are just a few questions you can start to ask yourself. Just jot them down on a piece of paper because you will come back to them later when you are updating your CV and crafting your speculative letter.

You can use your clout during your interview, retrieving relevant stories or a particular work experience that is not included in your CV. You can use your clout in your CV by including those achievements outside of work, or those gained from your experience of work. I'm a Chartered Marketer now, but that didn't happen until 2019 and it took me 6 years to achieve it, so now I have that string to add to my bow. It's another thing to add to my clout.

You can also produce a mind map of your journey thus far. (Google 'Mind Maps' if you don't know what they are). If you are on the creative side, I find mind maps really useful. This one below is an example from https://www.mindmeister.com/blog/students-guide-to-mind-mapping/

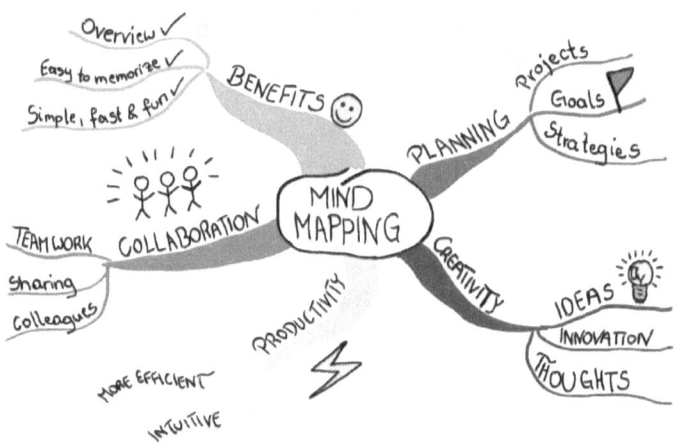

Once you have gathered your information around your life experiences, you can use your clout in your speculative letters as a 'hook' to help a potential employer gain interest in you.

I will explain all this in the next chapter using the **Career Cultivation C.H.A.R.T.**

6 CAREER CULTIVATION C.H.A.R.T.

The nitty gritty

I have been trying to lead you on the path of my journey thus far, to demonstrate to you how I got to where I am today and how you can too. You really can, don't give up, don't feel defeated by redundancy. Keep going.

The next part is about creating a speculative letter aimed at achieving the position you want at a company that you really want to work at. I've pulled together the essence of this into a system.

The system is called the **Career Cultivation C.H.A.R.T.**

The chart sections are broken down as follows:

C = Clout
H = Hook
A= Ambition
R = Research

T = Touchpoint

All of the points are used to help you cultivate a speculative letter that will accompany your standout CV. A CV that contains great firms and great brands. If your CV doesn't yet contain great firms and great brands, do not worry. This is a continual journey of improvement. you might be in your 20's or your 50's reading this mini-self helf guide. So tailor it to your particular needs and requirements.

If you are in your 20's and you realise after making your Mind Map, that you don't have much clout, then there is your first opportunity, go volunteer, take a free LinkedIn course, upskill!

If you are in your 50's, then you must have lots of life experiences that you can draw upon, but you might have been stuck in a perverbial rut! Break free and try this new approach.

Everyone else, I've already talked to you about clout with the aim of producing a mind map or list of things in your life that might help land you your next job. Clout is the C in C.H.A.R.T.

The next letter is H for Hook, but before that I would like to focus on A and R.

A = Ambition

Ambition is analysing where you want to be? In a physical sense, but also a strategic sense.

Physically - Are you willing to move home to secure your role? Or move abroad? If not, what is your search radius? How will you get to work? Is walking to work important to you, or are you happy to commute? Remote working (which is what I do) was on the rise before Coronavirus, but even more so post the big C. So now the world really can be your oyster.

But if you just want to work in one town or city, that is fine. Make that your footprint search area and stick to it. Often having a narrower focus helps with your search and with formulating your CV, having a wider focus geographically can obviously provide a wider range of options.

Strategically - What industry do you want to work in? Are there any firms in particular? What level are you looking to enter at? Would you enter at a lower level for a better role?

You remember early on, I said it is better to have a shit job at a great firm, than a great role at a shit firm. I said this because I know it to be true. People recruit people who have a good name/brand on their CV.

Yes, I know a great many people will disagree (particularly recruitment consultants). But I have tested this theory. I have applied for jobs using two different CVs. My real one (with good brands), and a fake one (with unknown brand firms). All other details (apart from my name etc) were identical. I never once had the dummy profile put forward for interview.

Another example: a person, who I will not name, prior to having a particular brand on his CV had applied for 167 jobs before he finally was offered one. After using the Career Cultivation C.H.A.R.T. and spending 12 months on an interim basis at an amazing firm, the next job search took 24 applications.

But do not worry, if you have unknowns or firms with poor brand images, there are still things you can do to improve your search and it starts with a great speculative letter.

Once you know your footprint or area of search, which in my case has nearly always been worldwide, but which in yours might just be Leeds or Brighton, and you know your strategy - manager level or lower - at let's say an Estate Agency Nationwide, the next part is the **R**. The **RESEARCH**.

R = Research

Research might well be obvious. But in order to pinpoint who you are going to target you need to have a list of potential employers. So start on Google and look to compile a spreadsheet of companies. I cannot emphasise enough how important it is to keep a spreadsheet (or if you are already CRM savvy, Zoho or other free CRM account). The reason to keep a log is so that you can gather consistent follow-up, record feedback, and in 3 or 4 years' time when you are looking again for your next move, you can remind yourself of who you had previously approached and what it was that they said.

It's also good to ask family and friends, old colleagues and use LinkedIn too to find out who might be hiring, or which firms are looking to grow.

Once you have compiled your list, put the companies in order of preference. Then look at each company's website and their latest press releases and, of course, their Careers sections. If there are no jobs advertised that fit you, don't worry because that is where your speculative letter comes in.

You have discovered your clout, you have your ambition mapped out, you have done your research and have a good list of contacts and you are raring to go. But what now?

It's a full time job, job-hunting. It keeps you awake at night, it tests your patience (waiting for recruiters to get back to you), it tests your mettle because nobody likes rejection and it tests your resilience because it can take time. And each time you apply, the amount of emotional effort required is quite substantial. So do yourself a favour and look after your health and wellbeing too!

Applying for jobs, or applying yourself in the pursuit of a job, career or new business is a full-time job in itself.

It's hard work job hunting. You get your hopes up, then you are literally ghosted by recruitment agencies; you apply direct, but then you never hear back. You see a job where you think you meet all the requirements, but then you don't even get an interview. It's downright demoralising!

Not to mention all the effort and enthusiasm you have to put into each application. So it's also important to look after yourself and your mental health. If you are unemployed, what better time to start walking, running, swimming etc, get back to nature and go and lie in that field and smell the grass, literally. Take care of yourself. Yes, I know we have to earn money, and you will again. But if you can, look after yourself too.

I'm a little guilty of failing to do this because I'm a grafter, a work-a-holic and a goal chaser, but in 2017 it all caught up with me, I was diagnosed with breast cancer. I was doing too much. I was trying to please everyone in my life, but I wasn't pleasing myself and I think the stress gave me cancer. You can read all about that in my book 'How to Rock Radiotherapy' and I'm better now, fingers crossed, but I don't know if it will return, so I am trying to live the best life I can.

This won't always make those who love me happy, but I cannot always please everyone and the minute you stop doing the same and start living your own life, the happier you will be. They say that a form of madness is trying to please all of the people, all of the time. Stop being a people pleaser and you will thank yourself for it in the long run.

T = Touchpoint

So you have your list of companies. Next you have to find out who the top person is, as well as the hiring manager and in many cases the gatekeeper (Secretary, PA). Basically the T in C.H.A.R.T. The aim here is a well-crafted letter to the CEO, MD or Managing Partner and copy in the hiring manager!

Yes, put pressure on that hiring manager (if there are any hiring managers on here that have been made redundant and looking for work, sorry, that's just the way the cookie crumbles).
It is important that you get the right touchpoint because you do not want your speculative letter falling under the radar, getting lost, or going to the wrong person. You want the decision maker, the person who has the budget to hire you.

You also need this person to be named where possible, so dont write to info@ or contact@ etc, you need a named person, because you WILL need to follow up. Rarely does your first attempt get a response. You have to bring out that resilience and keep trying.

I have found that by seeking out the decision maker, but copying in the head of x department, you are effectivley saying 'I want you to take notice, but I also respect the person to whom might be my line manager'. If you just and only write to the line manager they a) might not have the authority or the budget to hire you or b) feel threatened by you applying to be in their department. Are you after their job?

You need to find the balance and you may not get it right first time. You may also have to go via the gatekeeper (Secretary or PA) to get your speculative letter infront of the MD/CEO by obtaining an email address or asking them to forward it on. So always treat them with the respect they deserve. Do not dismiss them, make them your ally.

You have your list of companies, you know who you want to target, you know who at the firm you want to reach out to and you have done your research. What next?

H = Hook

Now you need to find the **H** in C.**H**.A.R.T. Your **HOOK**.

Your hook is a way to compliment the firm to which you are speculatively writing to. You might have found out they just won a business award for their charitable work. You might have done some chartiy work yourself and therefore you have a hook. Something in common or to admire. Something that get's their attention.

Or the firm might have mentioned that it is expanding with a new office in the town where you are looking at working. You could, therefore, write to say how well you know the area and their industry and could make new introductions for them. Bang, your hook!

Do you see where I am going here? Your speculative letter should not just be about all the wonderful things that you can bring to a job, but to compliment and show a deeper understanding of the firm or company to which you are applying.

Here is a real world example of one that I used. This is not made up, it's how it happened.

I mentioned earlier that after my divorce in the Cayman Islands, I flew back to Spain to stay with my mum while I decided what I would do next. Well, during that time, Mum and I flew back to the UK as she was relocating back to the UK and needed to speak to the Citizens Advice Bureau (CAB). We travelled back to a town (I won't name the town) and couldn't find the CAB office.

I saw there was a law firm, so I went in and asked the receptionist if she knew where the CAB was? The lady was so nice and so help-ful, she even got another receptionist to stand in for her while she pysically showed us where the CAB was.

The next day, I crafted my letter to the Managing Partner and cop-ied in the hiring manager. I explained that I had been so impressed by their receptionist and the impression it had left on me of their law firm and their brand, that it would stay with me for a very long time. So much so that it had prompted me to write to them directly seeking to be their next Marketing Director, in order that I could be part of that brand.

They were not looking for a Marketing Director, but I got an interview and, two more interviews later, I was offered a position there. Not only that, but the salary was more than I had ever earnt to that point and I was offered Marketing Director, when there was already a marketing team in place!

So, it can be done and you can do it too. You can, you just have to have the right mindset, the ambition and drive, the correctly-drafted letter and a hook that shows the person hiring that you really care about their firm.

Dont get me wrong, it takes time, effort, research and you have to be prepared for rejection or, worse, no response whatsoever. But if you don't put the effort in, each and every time, you will not get the reward you seek.

Here is another example: I wanted to make a return to the Cayman Islands around 2013 (notoriously difficult to find an open position there). None of the firms were hiring, so I contacted a connection I had on LinkedIn who used to work as a lawyer at the firm I worked for when I was there in 2007.

This person was now the Managing Partner of his own law firm out there. I started with a nice introductory LinkedIn request (If you are short on finances, get the free one month so you can use InMails). I then wrote to the Managing Partner explaining that I had spotted errors on their website and explained areas where I thought I could help. Of course I mentioned that I had worked at the largest firm on the island and a few conversations later I was offered a role as their Marketing Director. I didn't end up taking it in the end for one reason or another, but it proves you can get a job where none previously existed or was being advertised.

You just need a spot on speculative letter.

7. SPECULATIVE LETTERS

Real world examples

I have given you a couple of examples where I have used the speculative letter approach and I could provide more. But I don't want to make this all about me, I want you to start drafting your letter. This is about every single word you put down. Succinct sentences are best and to the point.

You can also use what I call the 'compliment sandwich', if you are trying to point out an error (i.e. something you could fix with your amazing skill set, like I did with the website example), then make sure you sandwich that between two compliments:

> *Wow Jane, the report you wrote last week was phenomenal, it really went down well with the clients. It didn't cover one essential element that I wanted to include, but I hope we can make that change in the next one I have lined up, which I am asking you to personally project manage. Would you like that repsponsibility?*

You see what I did there? And it's the same when crafting your speculative letter.

Below are some excerpts from letters of application, speculative letters and others. These are not all from my own experiences, but those I have crafted for others that have sought my help. Many refer to the legal industry as that is my background (legal marketing), but you can apply the same principles to your own industry, be it waitressing to stock broker.

Example 1

Working at board level in a complex matrix environment like a law firm has honed my ability to deal with the often conflicting requirements of each department and their client demands. I am told that I have a cool head and a natural gravitas that has enabled me to manage these relationships coupled with the ability to direct multiple projects with varying deadlines. I have led and managed high calibre worldwide teams, onsite and remotely, and was recently a finalist for the best business development team at The Lawyer, Management Awards 2013 [CLOUT]. I would like to continue this success with [company] and have noticed that your firm has never been shortlisted for an award [HOOK], which can, as you know, provide excellent kudos for the firm, a boost in moral for its employees and endless PR opportunities. I feel I excel at writing award entries and would be delighted to offer this as part of my application.....

Example 2

Professionally I am able to lead and inspire by example by taking a few bold steps, sticking to my decisions and seeing projects through to implementation. These attributes are what has made me a success in my career thus far, along with my ability to engage people and get the best out of the team [CLOUT]. I saw from a recent press release of yours that you had recruited a new partner in Employement Law, an area which you do not currently cover and I assume therefore are looking to expand into [HOOK]. I wonder if I might offer my experience of having covered employment law at a large global law firm and assist you in cross-selling this service to your existing clients. I have a ready-made formula for making that happen and I would be delighted to demonstrate this to you at interview.

Example 3

I recently saw that your company had invested in 2nd round of funding from [X Venture Capitalist Firm] with a view to expanding overseas with a new product [HOOK]. From a commercial standpoint, I have commoditised what is seen as a service-based industry into a product-based one [CLOUT]. The benefits in doing this within a service-led organisation are to enable the end user to see how their 'product' meets their needs and then to quantify it. Commercially-driven and entrepreneurial, I now manage my own business that I have developed from a seed idea into a fully functioning business, employing 3 members of staff and turning over in excess of £150k per annum. This commercial and business acumen are key strengths that I am able to bring to [company] in supporting the Managing Partner with the growth of [company].

Example 4

[COMPLIMENT SANDWICH] On a recent trip to Edinburgh I was reccommended to try your restaurant and was told it was the best Indian food money could buy. I have to agree, I received what can only be described as manna on a plate, but in addition the service I received was second to none. I did notice however, that there was a very large queue of people waiting to come in, and some people were being turned away. I am writing as I specialise in front of house and would like to offer my services to set up and manage your booking and front of house processes so that I can deliver and build upon your excellent reputation.

Your speculative letter should include the following elements.

1. A good title.

A good title is so important, because it gets the end user to actually open your email or letter. It can also be random or creative in order to get the end user to open your email. For example;

    a) Unique insight into [x] company
    b) Strategy for recruitment in marketing
    c) A way forward for growth
    d) Waitressing Wizard! A new standard in collecting cups!

Just something different than FAO Mr/Mrs Brown, CEO.

2. A good opening paragraph - get to the point, make it as interesting as possible.

Next comes the opening paragraph. This can be quite a tricky area, as you want to catch their attention enough to read the full email and your proposal without having to give it all away in the very first paragraph. You can include your 'hook' here or in the next paragraph.

> **a) Thanks for reading on. I saw your firm recently had expanded into the Reading area and in particular offering a new product which I happen to specialise in!**

> **b) I was scrolling through the top tech 100 and came across your firm - placed 98th - I'm excited to see you made the top 100, congratulations. I would like to be part of the team that takes you to No1, let me explain how......**

Its better to write something quite catchy and to the point instead of; Dear Mr Brown, I hope this email finds you well. I am writing in relation to any openings you might have at [X company].

3.   Explain how you, and only you, can solve their problem, or the problem you have identified.

This is the section of the letter or email where you have to find all your creative juices, add your clout and your hook, if you havent already used it in paragraph one. This is where you can expand on it.

> **a) I was recently a customer in your new Vegan cafe. When I asked the waitress for the ingredients in your veggie bake, she couldnt answer and I felt that she did not enjoy the food she was serving as her expression was one of disgust. My aim is not to get anyone into trouble, but I feel you could be losing customers with this lack of interest and energy.**

> **I said I was a Waitressing Wizard, well, in the case of Veganism, I am! I have spent the last 6 months in [Thailand] learning all the new ways to cook up vegan food. I'm**

not a chef, but I am so passionate about the food and about how the Thai people treat their customers and I would like to bring that to your cafe. I would be very happy to provide a 2 week unpaid trial to showcase my waitressing talent, so that you have nothing to lose, and everything to gain!

The 'hook' here is that you have acted as a mystery shopper, in effect. You have actually eaten at the cafe, you have experienced poor service and now you can use your 'clout' your experience in Thailand to get your foot in the door.

4. Ask for a call or follow up.

5. Follow up.

If you don't hear back, don't be afraid to follow up with a further email. Go to your sent items, find the email and forward it again to the same people with a message. Some people can get really creative here and make light of the fact that they haven't heard back. Or just show enthusiasm.

6. Follow up the follow up.

If you don't hear back from your second or third email, don't be afraid to follow up with a phone call.

I know, it's hard, but they can only say no! At best they can say yes. You are not calling to get the job there and then, you are just calling to get yourself to the next stage: a meeting, another call or some sort of informal interview. A phone call really shows you have courage and initiative and so even if they say, no, the blame is really on them for not answering your email in the first place!

7. Don't give up.

Even if it comes to nothing, keep this contact in your LinkedIn contacts, on your spreadsheet and front of brain, because you may well need them in 3,5 or 10 years' time when the next recession, plague or world -war 3 comes round.

8. Be you.

Be passionate, have energy, show a willingness to go beyond expectations and deliver. Even introverts like me can show energy, you don't have to have a bubbly personality or the type that can talk the hind leg off a donkey. Just be you, just an enhanced version. And if you are very introverted or shy, bite the bullet and fake it till you make it.

There are endless ways you can craft your speculative letter that stands out from the crowd. Go on, give it a go.

8. MORPHING

Changing you!

These days it doesn't have to be a letter. Although receiving a beautifully written letter these days is quite a nice thing to receive. It could be an email, even a video message, a LinkedIN connect request (for goodness sake, please personalise them!!).

Writing a letter is a skill. It is best to write from the heart, as you really are, much like I am writing this book. For me that means serious, but with a sense of humour.

Write your letter in your style, tailoured to your type of industry. If you are applying for a cake decoration post, why not send them a cup-cake with your speculative letter, or create a new recipe just for them? If you are a data analyst, put in clever charts to demonstrate your skill.
Don't be afraid to be different. I once heard a brilliant quote by George Bernard Shaw: "Life isn't about finding yourself; it's about creating yourself".

Morphing is about creating youself through self-improvement in order to get the job or career you want.

For example, if you want a job in marketing, but you missed the boat on going to university, then take some free courses on

LinkedIn and join the Chartered Institute of Marketing so you can add 'Member CIM' to your CV. Create a marketing plan for the firm you are trying to get a post at. You can download a template from Google these days. As a matter of fact, you can learn most things from YouTube and online these days, so don't be afraid to add new strings to your bows.

If you want to work in the tourism industry, but all you have done so far is office work, get a weekend job waiting tables in the nicest hotel you can find and learn on the job. Take mini courses online, there are hundreds out there.

I know morse code; I know how to shoot an automatic machine gun (gained during my RAF career); I know how to give CPR (I trained as a volunteer Community First Responder); I have arrested someone when I was a Special Constable (another volunteer role); I am a Chartered Marketer (I didn't attend university); I have written six books, a script, a novel and a children's book, none of which relate to my corporate career, other than being a Chartered Marketer, but I can use all those skills in some way in my career and, boy, do I have interesting stories to relay to any potential interviewer!

I am walking, talking living proof that you can achieve anything you set your mind to, if only you are willing to give it a go, step outside your comfort zones and try. As I said early on, nothing is going to fall into your lap, you have to work at it. You have to find your motivation.

This morphing can also work when you are looking at leaving one career altogether and perhaps thinking about starting your own business. Once you go through the 'clout' excercise, you may realise that the job you thought you wanted (chef in a pub) actually turns out to be wanting to own a boutique bed and breakfast!

Transformation, self-improvement is a lifetime, never ending goal. If you read my book 'How to Rock Retirement' you will see I talk about teaching 'old dogs new tricks'. This never ending self improvement, learning new skills starts young and should never end.

That book is all about empowering the older generation to try new things, educate themselves, step out of comfort zones. Never stop, never give up, keep trying new things and you will surprise yourself.

Morph yourself into who you want to be and don't settle for anything less. You ARE worth it, redundancy isnt the end.

9. GREENER GRASS?

The never ending quest

For me, I am someone on the eternal quest for change, for improvements in all aspects of my life (Don't worry hubby, I am very happily married). For some people this is not what they want, so to those people it would be incremental changes and self-improvements. Not everyone is geared to moving house, moving country at the drop of a hat. And I know some of you are more grounded and have a more still and peaceful life because always looking for greener grass can be exhausting, but fun! One day I may stop, but for now, I am enjoying the journey and I hope you do to.

It's a never ending quest, but that is what makes life so exciting. For me at least. We all have different forms of happiness, stillness, peace, joy. I don't know what makes me this way and you your way, we are all unique individuals. But I hope you find what you are looking for and I hope this book has helped you in some small way to find the job, career or path you need to get you back into work.

My aim has been to provide you with ideas on how to achieve this. Actionable goals that, when put together, can help you get the position you want, start a business, overcome redundancy or long term unemployment or any other change-inducing catalyst in your life. It's all about application. So stop applying for jobs and start applying yourself!

But, when you find that greener grass, chew on it a while, enjoy and savour the grass and, when you are full, move on.

10. GOALS MET

Score!

I mentioned in Chapter 1 that my first husband would say that the grass isn't greener. I would respond to that by saying that it may not be greener, but it is a different colour green, and I want to try all the variations, 50 shades of green?

In the same vein that beauty is in the eye of the beholder, one person's dream job - air hostess, for example - could be another person's nightmare - mine actually, as I secretly hate flying!

So, test the waters, test new waters and stretch yourself and your limits because you never know what you might find out about yourself and your own capabilities.

I hope that you recover from whatever catalyst you are facing right now and find the courage to move on. Take action from your redundancy or job loss. I hope that you seek out the role you want and get it, start that business or educate yourself to reach your goals. Make small achieveable goals, even if it is just get out of bed and have a shower, its one step closer to action. Don't be too hard on yourself. Just do SOMETHING!

I should probably explain what I meant by 'Stop applying for jobs and start applying yourself' on my Title page. This means that applying for endless jobs that you see on job boards, can be soul destroying. It can take hundreds of applications before you finally hit gold. I'm not saying don't do it, I'm saying that there might be a better way. By applying yourself and taking action, finding your clout and exploiting that, looking for a hook and finding the big fish, you will reap more rewarding results.

You could put all this effort into starting your own business, your own venture. Wouldn't that be great? What an achievement.

I would love to hear of your successes and achievements. You can reach me via www.amandanoblesimmons.com

To summarise:

1. Accept Change and cycle through GRIEF
2. Set an end Goal, then set mini goals to acheieve that
3. Adapt your mindset with PMA and the 6 Ps
4. Discover your CLOUT
5. Always have your CV prepared and up-to-date
6. Craft your speculative letter using C.H.A.R.T.
7. Enjoy the Grass

ACKNOWLEDGEMENT

I would not have been able to write this book had I not finally pulled my finger out of the preverbial and put finger to keyboard! Sorry were you expecting some gushing acknowledgements then? I'm joking, here they are.

In all seriousness, I couldn't have done any of my books without the support and love of my husband, Scott. He is a rock and safe harbour for me and the kids. He could probably write his own book 'How to Rock Relationships', because he is a wonderful husband and father.

To my four beautiful children: Phoebe, Fenella, Pippa and Guy. I hope I can make you proud of me. I have achived a great deal in my life, but none so much as being blessed with you horrible lot!

To my mum, Jennifer. My gypsy inspiration. I think I get my constant need for change and drive from you. We moved around a lot as kids. And I mean A LOT. But It made me who I am and I quite like myself. So thanks, and I love you.

My sister, Victoria, who has been there for me throughout all my ups and downs. How many laughing fits have we had together? Now that we have both turned 50, lets write that book about what it *really* feels like to turn 50, warts and all! 'How to Rock a Mid-Life Crisis' I feel coming on.

To the young man, who started a conversation with me, for no apparent reason, while I was queuing at Kentucky Fried Chicken at a service station one time. For restoring my faith in human beings (and young people)! I don't know who you were or why you talked to me, but it made a lasting impression. I hope to be more like you. (I'm and introvert who fakes it till she makes it!).

To all the future people who are not yet in my life, but whom I hope to connect with via this book. I look forward to inspiring you and to helping you achieve your moment of change. I'm an introvert: shy and never really fit in. So if I can do it, you can too.

Talk to me via www.amandanoblesimmons.com. I would love to hear about your transformation or small goal smashing.

ABOUT THE AUTHOR

Amanda Noble-Simmons

Amanda lives in a constant state of movement, so at the time of writing, she lives in Yorkshire, but is planning on moving back to Gibraltar. However, this could all change at the drop of a hat and it could be The Cayman Islands, Cornwall or who knows.......

Amanda is married to Scott and has four beautiful children, who are all talented in their own individual ways.

Phoebe is a talented artist, photographer and model see www.phoebenobleart.com

Fenella is about to start her A Levels and has plans to go onto University and study either Economics or Business.

Pippa is a clever girl of 8 who sings, writes her own songs, loves to be the centre of attention, so maybe one day she will be on the stage.

Guy is a cutey pie of 6 with a heart of gold. He loves truck films, kinetic sand and going on holiday with his family.

Amanda has her own Marketing and Business Development consultancy business www.legalbalance.co.uk and has written scripts, as well as other self help books which can also be purchased on Kindle.

She is a Chartered Marketer and has been shortlisted for a number of awards during her career.

All of Amandas' 'How to Rock..' series can be found at www.amandanoblesimmons.com

www.ingramcontent.com/pod-product-compliance
Lightning Source LLC
Chambersburg PA
CBHW030527220526
45463CB00007B/2753